SCRAMBLING FOR SURVIVAL

Scrambling for Survival

A Third Collection of Poems
written by Maggie May

Illustrated by
Al Turner

Published by The Royal Air Force Benevolent Fund Enterprises
Building 15, RAF Fairford, Glos GL7 4DL, England

ISBN 0 9516581 5 8

Typeset by Sue J. Bushell/Oxford Air Research

Printing and reproductions by Jade Productions, Room 1201, New
Way Centre, 415 Hennessy Road, Wanchai, Hong Kong.

FOR SALLY
my daughter-in-law,
who is now an RAF wife . . .

Contents

Air Force Games

It's five o'clock on Friday
And their working day is done
They drop into the Bar
(Well, they deserve a little fun)

All shattered chaps together
It's such *heaven* to unwind
And thoughts of a dear wife at home
Will never cross their mind,

And what about the game they play
When they go off each day?
They let us *guess* when they'll be home
– It's much more fun that way . . .

And every now and then
They take us out to have a jar,
To 'show us off' . . . and *wave* to us
Across a crowded bar!

But sometimes we can get dressed up
And have a bite to eat,
They bring us out and dust us off,
And tell us: "it's a *treat*",

How do they get away with it
And keep us suffering so?
And can we ever change them?
I fear the answer's "no" . . .

Introduction

When I was invited by the Royal Air Force Benevolent Fund to write a third volume about RAF wives, following *Waiting in the Wings* and *Posh Frocks and Postings*, I decided to add another dimension – the RAF mum.

The mothers among us will know only too well the wrench when the children start school, the agony of their exams and the emptiness when they finally "fly the nest". All this while coping with their father, who ensures that life continues as erratically as possible with countless "jollies", unforgettable dinners, bedroom-sharing with an unusual mistress, plus many more situations that never fail to keep us on our toes.

I have had much fun and nostalgia writing these poems and, as the title suggests, life is far from being a smooth ride the older we get and the further up the ladder we go!

Once again, my wholehearted thanks go to Al Turner who illustrated Scrambling for Survival so aptly with his sense of humour, and to my husband John and sons Simon and Jonathan who have inspired me to write about the bumpy ride through the RAF "Scramble".

Maggie May

Foreword

From Air Chief Marshal Sir Roger Palin KCB, OBE, MA, FRAeS, FIPM

Maggie May's first two anthologies were instant successes. Here is a third, which embraces the thrills, disasters, cares and despairs of being a mum as well as a wife. The first two struck many chords; hopefully this one will strike a few more and evoke a nostalgic tear or two as well.

The proceeds of the sales of all three editions have kindly been donated by Maggie to the RAF Benevolent Fund. Your purchase of this book, therefore dear reader, will contribute directly to the relief of need and distress among the RAF extended family. Thus, besides a wry smile here and maybe a tear or two there, you can also derive a warm feeling from having contributed to a thoroughly worthy cause.

Controller
Royal Air Force Benevolent Fund

Happy Landings

No-one ever said this life would be a piece of cake,
And no-one warned you just how much a wife would have
   to take . . .
You see him in his uniform and fall for manly chest,
The rugged chin, the dashing looks – no wonder you're impressed,

Living in the Mess, he says, is such a lonely life
And soon he's had enough and feels it's time to take a wife,
He'll tell you that it's grim to prop the bar up every day
(You'll notice, though, that once he's wed he just can't stay away!)

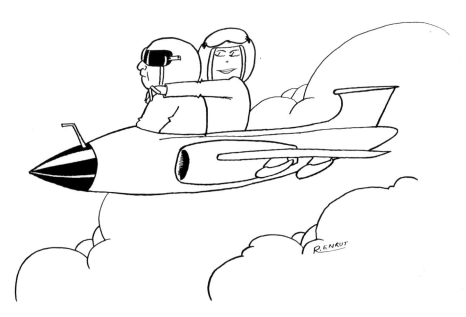

And hold tight – it's a bumpy ride

So you become an air force wife, he sweeps you off your feet
And whisks you to a spot that's not renowned for sun and heat,
Far away from Mother it's a strangely rural life
Your draughty quarter lets in winds that cut you like a knife,

But just as you've got used to quirky boiler and the draughts
He's posted – so you pack the house (it's not a load of laughs)
And when you leave your quarter there's a thing called 'marching out'
(Tell 'civvy' wives what happens and they all just fall about!)

You're often left alone if he goes off to fight a war
(But no point feeling too fed up, it's what his job is for)
Then when he's been away for weeks and life has seemed like hell
He'll come back full of lust . . . and bring his laundry bag as well!

Your life is full of parties (great excuse to buy a dress)
You'll go to summer balls and Ladies Guest Nights in the mess,
And though at times you feel as though you're going up the wall
You must admit at other times you're never bored at all . . .

It's clear his job comes first and it will keep you on your toes
You grit your teeth and go with him – no matter where he goes,
To lead this crazy life you summon all the strength you can
– Just hold tight, it's a bumpy ride . . . so stand by your man!

Bedlam at Breakfast

I often think that mornings
Should be gentle, calm . . . and hushed,
A time to unfold slowly
Absolutely nothing rushed,

I like to sip a cup of tea
While lingering through the post
And hate the loud intrusions of:
"Hey, Mum, is there more toast?"

I often think that mornings should be gentle, calm . . . and hushed

I'm bombarded by their questions
Such as, What Does God Look Like?
Or, Where Do Babies Come From?
And, Can I Fix Their Bike?

My nerves go snap, pop, crackle,
I'm more scrambled than the eggs –
They've hoovered up the orange juice
And left me . . . just the dregs,

The bacon has more sizzle
Than I can muster up
I make a constant flow of tea
(But hardly get a cup)

There's commotion in the bathroom
And it looks like they'll be late
(I feel I've done a full day's work
At twenty five past eight)

But when the little darlings
Have rushed out through the door
And you're left to sort the shambles
. . . What else are mothers for?

You always leave things to the very last minute!

Off on a Jolly

There's a great pile of stuff on the landing
(You'd think we'd been hit by a bomb)
But you're off with the chaps on detachment tomorrow
– And right now I wish that you'd *gone*!

I'm up to my eyes in the housework
But I'll stop what I'm doing (what's new?)
To wait on you hand, foot and finger, my love,
The way you're expecting me to,

Yes, I'll sew on the button that's missing
And sort all your socks into pairs
Then I'll iron those two shirts, find your old pair of shorts
And pick up these things on the stairs:

You'd love some more tea? – well, why not, dear?
I've only made *six* cups so far
(And if I have mine with a Valium or two
Things won't seem as fraught as they are)

It's not the detachment I mind, dear,
It's just all this *panic* I hate,
You *always* leave things to the very last minute
And get me worked up in a state . . .

At this rate you'll never be ready
(I wish I were going instead)
But this time tomorrow, as soon as you've gone,
The house will seem . . . horribly dead.

You'll fly off to some little 'hot spot'
(And protest that it's tough as can be)
It's a 'jolly' for you – I know only too well
. . . But not jolly at all, dear, for me!

He doesn't seem thrilled to be going

Letting Go

His bottom lip's starting to tremble,
He won't let me do up his tie –
We've mislaid a sock and my eye's on the clock
(Any minute he's going to cry)

He doesn't seem thrilled to be going
Now the 'Big Moment' is here,
No time to delay . . . get it over, I say,
But I'm in for a battle, I fear:

He says there's a pain in his tummy
And he's tucking himself up in bed!
He's giving me hell but looks fine, I can tell,
I am *dreading* the journey ahead . . .

He's pleading with me not to send him
And he's wound himself up in a state,
Will we get through the door? (I can't take much more)
What on *earth* will he do at the gate?

The playground is coming in sight, now
(I must stay in control and keep cool)
But how can you know what it's like letting go
At that moment your infant starts school?

What Shall I Wear?

We've had this invitation
To cocktails in the Mess
But I can't make my mind up
– A skirt and blouse . . . or dress?

My velvet jacket's just the thing
(But could be much too hot)
Or what about the baggy one,
I like the style a lot . . .

I've not a thing to wear!

But no – that's more for day wear,
They'll be dolled up, I bet,
In silks and polyesters
(Like all the 'well-heeled' set)

I could wear that new tunic
But then – which skirt to wear?
My lace one? Or the chiffon?
Or that mini, if I dare!

The blouse I bought last Tuesday
Would be the thing I'm sure,
But it's a bit too 'see-through'
Have I something more demure?

Perhaps that dress in turquoise?
But – I haven't shoes that go,
My two-piece? Wore it Friday night . . .
Oh dear, I just don't *know*:

What do they wear for drinks these days?
(Bet no-one's wearing boots!)
I could turn up in "glitter"
While they're in smart tweed suits . . .

There's only one thing for it,
I've just no choice, I *swear,*
I'll have to go out shopping
. . . I've not a *thing* to wear!

Cutting Corners

When a wife has to cope with a March Out
She can reach a quite desperate state,
And then drastic measures are called for
Due to having too much on her plate:

She worries she'll never be finished
With all of the jobs still to do
(Oh if only the Families Office
Could know what she has to go through!)

The following tale is a true one
Of a poor Air Force wife under stress,
As she stood in the midst of her bathroom
Surveying the whole sorry mess,

Just watch out for those who've cut corners!

24

The ceiling light needed unscrewing
And scrubbing, from what she could see,
The taps – a good clean up and polish
So this called for a nice cup of tea . . .

The window was covered in mildew
– The dust on the pelmet so thick,
And as for the grime on the bathtub,
She'd have to do something – and *quick*!

The ring round the tub was horrendous
(How on earth could the bath get this bad?)
She looked at her watch in a panic
– This could take all the time that she had.

Later, the quarter was ready
With bathroom all shining and bright
And she hoped that her trick with the bathtub
Would pass the inspection all right . . .

★ ★ ★ ★ ★ ★

Next day the new people moved in there
And as boxes were brought up the path
The new wife had one great desire
. . . A lovely long soak in the bath,

She looked at the newly-cleaned bathroom
And saw the bath gleamingly white
(Unaware of the previous panic
And how she was in for a fright)

The hot soapy water was soothing
(She was feeling so tired she felt faint)
Then she shrieked . . . for her skin had changed colour –
The bath had been *coated in paint*!

This shows the lengths some wives will go to
And in case this should happen to you,
Just watch out for those who've cut corners
On the day that the March Out is due.

Hooray for the Holidays

School holidays . . . your heart is sinking,
Can we stand it? mums are thinking
Constant noise and squabbles too –
"Mum, will you take us to the zoo?"

Never mind what plans *you've* made
In just one week your nerves are frayed;
It's raining and they're feeling bored
. . . The toy shop, what can they afford?

When do they go back to school?

They want the most expensive toy
And how you hate to squash their joy . . .
Steering them to cheaper rack
Is an art you seem to lack,

Distraction – that's the thing to do,
You offer drink, a bun or two
They head for snack bar licking lips
And say – they fancy egg and chips!

You get through cash in steady flow
And ask yourself 'where does it *go*?'
You've hung the washing on the line
They're in the garden, things look fine

But suddenly the football's *there*
On those clean clothes! You tear your hair,
The dreaded ice cream van comes round
(Why can't it sneak up without sound?)

You flop with jangling in your ears
When in they rush, the little dears –
You won't admit you've lost your cool
. . . But *when* do they go back to school?

The Plodders and the Dashers

While supermarket shopping
As that pile of food you stash,
Have you ever noticed
Those who plod – and those who dash?

You'll recognise a Dasher
For she nearly runs you down
She tears from aisle to aisle
With her face set in a frown,

To her it's so frustrating
When she buys the weekly fodder
To find the very shelf she wants
. . . Is blocked off, by a Plodder!

Now Plodders can't imagine
Why people have to dash,
They saunter round quite unaware
They're causing teeth to gnash:

Plodders often shop in pairs
So they can have a natter
And if it's near the Fruit and Veg
It surely doesn't matter?

A Dasher always shops alone
She has no time to chat,
While Plodders like to note the price
This week, on this and that . . .

A Dasher steers her trolley
Over toes, she doesn't mind –
To her the shop's a racecourse
And she won't be left behind!

She dashes for the deep freeze
To quickly grab a pizza
But finds a bunch of Plodders
Plus a trolley jam that greets her . . .

The Plodders duck for cover
(They've met her type before)
They can't see what the rush is,
They just like a good old jaw

A Dasher piles her trolley high
And nearly breaks her neck
And when she's reached the checkout
She's become a nervous wreck –

Next time that you go shopping
Just watch the things you do,
A Plodder . . . or a Dasher,
Which one, d'you think, is you?

You'll recognise a Dasher!

Why can't my Dad do something important

Craig's Dad

I saw Craig in the playground today, Mum,
And I said he could come here for tea
His dad's in the Air Force like my dad
And they live near the Naafi you see,

Craig's dad drives people around, Mum,
In a big shiny car while they chat,
I told him my dad is a pilot
. . . But he didn't say much about that.

Craig's dad is a Corporal, he told me,
(That's higher than my dad, I bet)
And he stands at the gate with a *rifle*!
– I said my dad's not got one . . . yet;

Craig's dad can stop an intruder
If one should pop out from the woods,
Well *my* dad flies *missions*, I told him,
And Craig said that's *almost* as good,

Craig's going to take me to see him
– He's on gate guard tomorrow, he said,
And he does a dead brilliant salute, Mum,
And he wears a tin hat on his head;

The thing is – when your dad's a pilot
You can't show him off to your mates . . .
Why can't *my* dad do something *important*
Like stand with a gun at the gates?

Without even a glimpse of suspenders and all
. . . You're flopped in the chair fast asleep!

Scant Hopes

We're off to the Dinner this evening
– I'm feeling relaxed, can't you tell?
And we're ready on time with no row for a change
And you've noticed my outfit as well . . .

I'm wearing a stunning new Number
(Don't ask where the housekeeping's gone!)
And I'm dicing with death with what's on underneath
(You will notice, I hope, later on!)

I feel quite romantic, I warn you,
So let's make this a really good night
Will you give me a bit of attention for once
And promise you won't get too tight?

Much later, we sit at the table
With a wonderful meal on the plate,
And I'm feeling lightheaded, on top of the world,
When you suddenly mouth: "You look great" –

You order some beer after dinner
Then stand with the chaps, right on cue,
(Well, if scanty black lace can't entice you away
There isn't much more I can do . . .)

Back home, I feel sure there'll be Romance
– But when I turn round I could *weep*,
Without even a *glimpse* of suspenders and all
. . . You're flopped in the chair fast asleep!

Your sock has a hole in the toe

Failed as a Mother

I feel I have failed as a mother
When
The vicar has popped in for tea
And I can't hear
A word
He is saying
— For you're both glued to children's TV

I feel I have failed as a mother
As
I limp home at twenty to two
And no-one
Has bothered
To fix any lunch
. . . Doesn't *one* of you know what to do?

I feel I have failed as a mother
If
To shoe shop we urgently go
When the saleslady
Pulls off
Your tatty old trainers
Your sock . . . has a hole in the toe:

I know I have failed as a mother
For
Tonight I served Hollandaise sauce,
The guests
Look impressed
As you help with the meal
— Till you laugh: "It's from Tesco, of course!"

Don't Tell Your Dad

At forty seven Canberra Crescent
– Nine o'clock one morning –
A rather tatty van drew up
A workman got out, yawning,

He knocked at number forty seven
(Fiddling with his sleeve)
The wife said: "Were you due today?
I'm just about to leave . . ."

No putting off the job, now

"Oh yes," he said, "I've come to trim
The bottom off yer door,
An' while I'm 'ere I'll see what's what
Then go an' get me saw . . ."

He then came in and looked around
To find out what was wrong
He told the lady: "Don't you fret
This job won't take too long,"

He went out softly whistling
And rummaged in his van
Then came back with a doleful look
(For such a cheerful man)

"You won't *believe* what's up, love,
I must be out me mind!
– I used me van, last night, see
And . . . left me tools – be'ind!"

That morning, it just happened,
Little Johnny was around,
At ten years old he knew just where
His dad's saw could be found:

He fetched it from the garage
As his mother gave a groan,
Then waved around this pride and joy
As though it were his own –

His mother looked quite worried
(The carpenter did too,
No putting off the job, now,
He knew what he must do)

So he took the saw in both hands
And winking at the lad
He said to Johnny: "Mum's the word,
. . . Best not tell your dad!"

One Skirt is Never Enough

I couldn't resist it, and truly I tried,
– This super skirt leaped out at me,
In floaty black chiffon, with beads at the hem,
It would suit me a treat, I could see . . .

Without hesitation I purchased the skirt
(I would wear it for dinner next week)
Then rushed home to try on the rest of the gear
And was thrilled – the whole outfit was *chic*:

But then I discovered I needed a belt
(They'd had matching ones there in the shop)
So back in I went . . . but they'd sold the last one
– Undeterred, I would 'shop till I drop'.

I found one at last, black satin with beads,
But back home it didn't look right . . .
It pulled in the skirt, the beads might rub off
And worse still, it felt rather tight,

So next morning I made a trip back to the shop
And handed back belt with dismay,
(I was feeling quite thrifty, with money in hand,
Till I saw something *else* on display)

As I passed a shop window of knitwear and tweeds
A *gorgeous* warm jumper I spied,
In colours I loved – and so cosy and bright,
Within seconds I'd hurried inside,

Snuggling into this big chunky knit
I knew I'd be mad not to buy
And I'd *never* grow tired of a garment like this
. . . I just had to have it, or die!

It would suit me a treat, I could see . . .

Back home I grabbed skirt I was certain would go
But, alas, it looked wrong (I was vexed)
Can you *believe* – not a single skirt matched
. . . So three guesses what I'm buying next!

So I really must put in more effort

Guilt among the Gingerbread

I frequently feel rather guilty
When reading in some magazine
About capable ladies who sparkle
At all kinds of fancy cuisine:

They make chutney and jam in abundance
So cheaply – with flavour divine,
While in our house no plum has been pureed
Because somehow I never have time . . .

No doubt wonderful gingerbread cookies
Emerge from their ovens, so neat,
(Well, that's not my scene I can tell you
– Just to open a packet's a treat)

And some are incredibly clever
At lacemaking, knitting and such,
They must save their husbands a fortune
(I don't seem to have the right touch)

But the last word in thrift, I've decided,
Is saving those old laddered tights
And knitting them up into hearthrugs
And place mats, or other delights!

They're more dedicated than I am,
Those ladies who beaver away,
So I really must put in more effort
And try it . . . some other day.

In the Hot Seat

When you're asked if you'd like to be Chairman
You feel you can hardly refuse,
And you hope it's a job you can handle
For it's not a position you'd choose . . .

You then meet the Wives Club committee
Whose keenness exceeds your belief
(As you warily smile round the table
You pray you won't get too much grief)

It's not a position you'd choose . . .

You may find when on a committee
Of women assembled in force
That you're 'shot down in flames' – fairly often –
People tell you it's par for the course:

But this group appears to be friendly
And they're looking to you, you can tell
So you inwardly feel rather grateful
That everything's working out well,

A Ladies' Lunch now is debated,
Which speaker will go down a treat?
And how many guests, and what menu
And who's to be in 'the hot seat'?

The President says she'd prefer it
If she could duck out of this do
So there's only one person in question
. . . And it's not hard to guess that it's *you*!

You inwardly groan at the prospect
Of having to stand up and speak
(And you won't feel like eating a *morsel*
And you'll worry about it all week . . .)

But at lunch you grab hold of the gavel
And bang it like never before –
In an instant all eyes are upon you
And you wish you could sneak through the door,

As you stand there addressing the ladies
And notice the smiles on each face
You relax . . . for there could be no other
Who'd wish she were there in your place . . .

So along came the men with their ladders

44

Along came the PSA . . .

"We hear you've a snag with your ceiling,"
Said the men from the PSA,
And they gazed at the patch in the corner
Saying: "This should be done – right away."

They'd come when the quarter was empty
The two weeks before we moved in,
(And to think we believed they would *do* it,
We should know that these chaps always win)

Suffice it to say, when we moved in
The great flaking patch was still there!
But the PSA rushed to assure us
It was pressure of work – they despair . . .

They'd been *overwhelmed* with their jobsheets,
But ours was now Job Number One,
So along came the men with their ladders
"In no time we'll have this job done":

But instead of the promised *new* ceiling
They slapped on a clumsy great patch
(So much *quicker*, and so much less effort
Than starting the whole thing from scratch)

PSA came back and promised
This time *proper job* would be done,
So once more the lounge was dismantled
And furniture piled up . . . what fun,

Well, no-one turned up on the Monday,
On Tuesday at last came the van
But instead of three workmen to do it
– PSA had sent only one man.

"An urgent job's come up". he told us
"But they'll be here at lunchtime, you'll see,
So I'm going to start – in a jiffy –
When I've brewed up a nice cup of tea . . ."

The job was eventually started
And they stripped off the paper that day
. . . But the ceiling collapsed – in great pieces!
So they fled without further delay:

Then plasterers had to be summoned
And carpet was whisked through the door,
They brought in some large trestle tables
(Could we put up with anything more?)

Five days it took for the plaster
Then two days to paint, in the end,
(But if only they'd done it the first time
We needn't have gone round the bend . . .)

We now have a lovely smooth ceiling
Much admired by those PSA men
– But I hope they don't hear of this poem
Or they might come and call here again!

The Waiting Game

One glance at his face tells the story –
Tomorrow we'll all know the worst,
When the dreaded 'A' level results will come out
(Right now I'm so tense I could *burst*)

If only we knew that he'd passed them!
Oh just to know that would be bliss,
All those hours at his books (was he having us on?)
I just hate being worried like this,

I'm trying to laugh and be cheerful
And suggesting some place we could go,
But he wants to stay up in his bedroom and flop
(I don't think I've seen him this low)

At dinner we must look a picture
As we're all staring down at the food,
And no-one is hungry, or saying a word
For tonight we're just not in the mood . . .

Nana's rung up feeling anxious
– Her stomach is playing up too
And she says she can guess at the agony here
(Oh the things that we mothers go through)

I'm longing to give him a cuddle
To help take the tension away
But soon we'll be out of this frightful suspense
. . . So roll on tomorrow, I say!

Balancing Act

I've just had a letter this morning
(The first in two weeks, I might add)
He says everything's fine out in Cyprus
And the weather's the best that they've had . . .

Right now I could *scream* with the children
– They've been running me ragged for days
(It's always the same without Father
They go through a "give-mum-hell" phase!)

But I'll still play my role of 'The Juggler'

His letter was full of the flying
And he's thinking about us, he said,
But no word of his darling son's birthday
I think it's gone out of his head:

I've masses to do for the party
(Great timing – he'll miss all *that* fun)
I'll have nine rowdy kids scoffing jellies
While he's far away in the sun,

I'm due to see teachers this evening
(That's *another* event he will miss)
And I'll have to check up on the sitter
– Why can't *he* handle something like this?

They're supposed to be doing their homework
But they're lounging in front of TV
And I haven't the strength for a battle
– I'm in need of a nice cup of tea,

In four weeks his trip will be over
So they'll love seeing Daddy appear
But I'll still play my role of 'The Juggler'
. . . So nothing will change much, I fear!

Survival of the Fittest

I don't know how long I can keep up this pace
For tonight, once again, I'm hostess;
We've been out every night, now it's dinner for ten
(It's about time I had a new dress!)

The chap on my right is hard work, I can tell you,
I'm not getting through, that's for sure,
But I reckon it's time to bring in the next course
So I'll do a quick dash through the door . . .

If only she knew what this life's really like

The puds are passed round and they're all tucking in
– Dare I undo my skirt? Oh why not . . .
And I've kicked off my shoes (not the done thing I know
But right now – I don't care a jot)

My husband's absorbed in deep conversation,
He's not even looking my way
And he doesn't seem nearly as tired as I feel
(But he's not done what I've done today)

I never imagined how draining it is
With these functions that last half the night,
All this clutching a drink with fixed smile on my face
– And hoping I won't get too tight.

So I'm here in the midst of these glamorous guests
With sleep my immediate thought,
When my husband announces the time has now come
For the chaps to indulge in the port . . .

I lead all the ladies upstairs for a break
(At this point things often seem flat)
But the bedroom's a *tip* so I'm rushing around
Stuffing clothes here and there while we chat,

One of the wives says it must be amazing
To live in such elegant style,
(If she only knew what this life's *really* like!
But I nod my head brightly and smile)

We move down the stairs for the coffee and mints
As the chaps wander in from the hall,
And right now I'm thinking: a *fabulous* night . . .
And tomorrow? No problem at all . . .

A Man's World

It's terribly one-sided
In this family of mine
With three great strapping menfolk
To try to keep in line . . .

I don't know how they do it
But they seem to get their way
And hardly ever listen
To anything I say!

*It's good to have three chaps around
When spiders are about . . .*

And when it's sport they're watching
On the jolly old TV
They never think there might be
Something else I'd like to see,

Of all the programmes on it
They love cricket most of all
(I simply cannot fathom
All this fuss about a ball)

They mutter things like "googlies"
And strain to read the score,
They never even notice
When I've gone and slammed the
    door.

If I keep them fed and watered
They are quietly content
(I live in hope they'll wait on me
Oh what a rare event!)

But sometimes in the bathroom
If they hear me scream and shout
It's good to have three chaps around
When spiders are about . . .

Or if I've done the shopping
And it's all a bit too much
I smile and sweetly tell them:
"That lot needs a strong man's touch"

So if I'm really honest
– Though at times it drives me mad –
I've come to the conclusion
Being outnumbered's . . . not so bad.

They'd bring home little gems made from an egg box

Paintings on the Cupboards

Mothers never give up being mothers
You struggle through those early frantic days
And when your children reach the age of twenty
They seem to need you more, in many ways . . .

You think back to the time when they were tiny
And rushed like little rockets through the door,
While throwing down their school bags on the table
They'd spread their bits of Lego on the floor,

You queued for Disney films when it was raining
(The kids today want smarter things than that)
And ketchup and fish fingers were their favourite
And they'd snuggle on your knee and have a chat:

They'd bring home little gems made from an egg box,
Binoculars from loo rolls – just for you!
And you'd proudly pin their paintings on the cupboards
(And kid yourself you'd reared a Rembrandt, too)

And then one day you blink and they're enormous –
Their great long legs are sprawled across the floor
And scattered socks and books on bedroom carpet
Replace the cars and train sets from before,

They drape themselves in every corner, loudly,
Monopolising TV, fridge and 'phone,
And you wonder where those infant days have gone to
And you marvel at the rapid way they've grown . . .

And when you stand and look around the kitchen
With cupboard doors bereft of works of art,
You still can see those precious little paintings,
Bold and clear . . . and locked inside your heart.

Auntie's Place

There are times in my life when I long for
A nice little undisturbed spot
Away from demands of a husband and kids
Where cooking and chores there are not . . .

Let me tell you, I found a real haven
When I visited Auntie last week,
Her living room, comfy and cosy,
Had all the attractions I seek:

Then Auntie passed round buttered crumpets

Her TV was tuned to a programme
Not racing or cricket – no fear!
It was one of those old-fashioned movies
Where women might shed the odd tear,

No sudden intrusions to spoil it,
No menfolk tuned in to the sport,
So it felt very strange just to wallow
In womanly films of this sort.

Then Auntie passed round buttered crumpets
We had tea in best cups on a tray
(What a change from my *usual* Sundays
Rushing round in the thick of the fray)

For Auntie has never been married,
She does just whatever she likes
And she's *never* knee-deep on a Sunday
With football boots, skateboards and bikes!

It's soothing to flop on her sofa
And chat while you're watching TV
What bliss . . . not to make endless cuppas
But have somebody cosseting *me*:

Yes, Auntie's place truly is heaven
– Can't say where she lives, that's for sure
For then she might find – every Sunday –
There'd be mums queuing up at her door!

The Briefcase

You've come through the door with your briefcase
And set it down neatly I see –
Making sure no-one kicks or disturbs it at all
(It gets far more attention than me)

It's tucked by your side on a journey
And you give it a pat now and then
It holds all your secrets so staunchly within
– It's a friend when you're with other men:

It's even been brought to our bedroom

It's even been brought to our bedroom
When you can't let it out of your sight
(But so far it hasn't come into our *bed*
When it does . . . what an interesting night!)

When sharing the back seat together
Being driven to airport one day,
You suddenly plonk down the briefcase between us
"You don't mind too much, dear?" you say,

I can hardly object, since it's normal
When sharing the back seat with you
To sit down with something that's tough and unbending
And doesn't say much . . . so what's new?

But tonight there's not *one* case but *two*, dear
So I don't stand a chance, I can see . . .
Who'd have thought that a straight-sided mistress like this
Would come between my man and me?

So set off with hope
On this latest adventure

A New Page of Your Life

I wish you could know
How I feel at this moment
As you begin the next stage of your life,
Cheerful and brave
Yet gentle and wary
Nineteen years old . . . a new page of your life

All that you are
I shall gratefully treasure
Your honesty, humour – your twinkling smile,
And as I look back
On the years of your childhood
You were becoming this man all the while

So set off with hope
On this latest adventure
Places are beckoning, people to meet;
And there isn't a mother
Prouder than me
As I'm waving you off with the world at your feet.

So thank you for kindly agreeing
For two years to give up your life

The Letter We Never Receive

Dear Mrs Bloggs

Regarding your husband's promotion,
His posting's the 'high profile' sort
And we hear you'll be happy to join him, of course,
And give him your usual support.

He'll need to take up his appointment
Exactly twelve weeks from today
– Did you know that it's partly *your* marvellous efforts
That pointed this posting his way?

We're *sure* you won't mind the upheaval
Of moving again rather soon
And we feel – once you're used to the climate up there –
That you're going to be "over the moon".

We're fully aware of your feelings
In giving up home and career,
And, truly, we're glad you'll be there by his side
– What else is a wife for, my dear?

We hardly need mention we're grateful
For wives must come first, we agree,
And we'd like you to know we'll go *out of our way*
To make things as smooth as can be.

So thank you for kindly agreeing
For two years to give up your life
We'd expect nothing less from a lady like you
Who's a wonderful RAF wife . . .

Yours obligingly,